Chinese Fables & Wisdom

Insights for Better Living

Chinese Fables & Wisdom
Insights for Better Living

By Tom Te-Wu Ma

Barricade Books, Inc.

Published by Barricade Books Inc.
150 Fifth Avenue
Suite 700
New York, NY 10011

Library of Congress Cataloging-in-Publication Data

Ma, Tom.
    Chinese fables and wisdom : insights for better
    living / by Tom Ma.
         p.   cm.
    Originally published: Lake Worth, FL :
    Gardner Press, 1996.
      ISBN 1-56980-123-1
      1. Fables, Chinese. 2. Wisdom—Anecdotes.
    I. Title.
    PN989.C5M3 1997
    398.2'0951—dc21   97-29987
                                 CIP

Contents

The Farmer and the Ox

Before machinery was used for agriculture in China, farmers had to do almost everything by hand. They used simple tools with the help of some animals, mostly cattle. An ox or cow in the early days was always a Chinese farmer's most intimate working partner.

One young Chinese farmer had an ox that was left to him by his deceased parents, together with a small old house and some acres of land. Since he had no brother or sister, he lived by himself He took care of the ox, cooked for himself, and did all the other necessary household chores.

Every day he hoped he could finish the work in the field as early as possible, so he could have more time to go shopping. Therefore, he often whipped the ox to go faster when he arrived in the field. The frequent, unreasonable whips angered the ox. The ox was old and had done his best, yet he had to endure the cruel whippings every day. To resist the tyrannous treatment, the ox purposely walked more slowly instead of faster. Consequently, the animal received more whips, and the work in the field went on more slowly than the farmer expected.

The young farmer complained that he must have bad luck to own the laziest ox in the world. The ox murmured that he must have the worst fate to have the worst master in the world. They hated each other. They did not cooperate with each other, but they had to work together.

One summer afternoon, the sunshine made the fields burn and caused workers to easily lose their temper. The farmer kept whipping the ox to go faster, but the ox still walked very slowly. The more the farmer whipped, the slower the ox was and the angrier they both became in the burning sunshine.

Accidentally, maybe purposely, the ox suddenly fell down upon the ground. It had never happened before, but it happened that day. The ox said to himself that he had suffered enough from the cruel master. He would rather die than endure the painful whippings. So, he closed his eyes and lay still in the field waiting for death.

The strange, unexpected incident frightened the young farmer. He had no experience to manage such an emergency. He sat down beside the dying animal. Suddenly he realized the importance of the ox. Without the animal, how could he work in the field totally by himself? The more he thought, the more frightened he became.

Finally, he hugged the animal and cried loudly. After a while, he noticed the animal was still breathing. He immediately gave the ox water to drink and some fresh grass to eat. Gradually, the ox opened his eyes. Then the ox stood up slowly. The man was so excited that he jumped and hugged the ox again and again. With such affectionate care, the ox decided to go back to work. But the man quit the job for the day and took his animal home early to rest.

From that day on, the farmer did not whip his ox anymore. He fed the ox as often as the animal desired. He hugged the ox to show his appreciation every time he quit work and was ready to go home.

The ox was happy. He walked as fast as he could. He told himself that he was the luckiest ox in the world, for he had the best master. Meanwhile, the farmer could go home earlier every day, so he was happy, too. He told his friends he was so lucky to have such a nice ox.

This is a world of love. Hate causes only more unpleasantness or misery, and many things become worse. If you treat others with love, you will get the same in return. It works between a man and an animal. It should work among human beings, too. 🐾

Traps behind the Leaves

A cicada is an insect with a broad head and membranous wings, commonly seen in the summer in most parts of China.

The male cicada has a pair of resonating organs that produce a high-pitched drone. Hundreds of cicadas singing together create music that is quite pleasant. The chorus of cicadas is one of the interesting things I often miss about my homeland. As a child, I had no school in the summer. I liked to lie under the trees with a few companions, doing nothing but enjoying the happy cicadas' chorus half a century ago at our farm.

There is a story about a cicada in the Chinese classic, *Chuang-Tzu*. Once upon a time, a male cicada joyfully joined his friends in singing the most beautiful praises of happy summer. He sang and sang, completely intoxicating himself in the comfortable, hot afternoon without noticing a great danger approaching.

A couple of inches away, behind the singer, was a huge mantis extending his two powerful sawlike forelimbs, preparing to make a sudden attack on the helpless cicada. The mantis was concentrating on how to catch the delicate cicada for his late lunch and did not realize that a hungry yellow bird was hiding under the leaves, less than half a foot behind the mantis.

The bird was sure he could capture the mantis for his early supper, but he never dreamed that a mischievous boy under the branches was aiming at him with his handmade bow. When the boy got the bird, the boy jumped excitedly and hurt himself by a careless fall as he stepped into a hole in front of him.

What the author tried to tell us is that if you think you are smart enough to take advantage of another person, there is always somebody else who might be smarter than you, trying to take advantage of you. The self-declared smartest person often becomes the victim of an unexpected accident.

There are traps behind leaves and under branches. As long as you do not take advantage of someone else, you will be smart enough to defend yourself. 🦋

The Snipe and the Clam

A clam was enjoying the sunshine by a river one beautiful day. She opened her two shieldlike shells toward the lovely sun and forgot about all her troubles with the others in the river.

Suddenly, a hungry pin-tailed snipe dropped from the blue sky, stuck his long, sharp bill into the shells and tried to nip the lovely pink flesh for his quick lunch. Right at this moment, the clam closed her shells very tightly and clasped the bird's bill as hard as she could. The snipe did not get what he wanted and tried all he could to pull back his beak, but in vain. Both stiffened with anger, and neither would concede. The two parties were at a deadlock.

"If it does not rain tomorrow or the next day, there will be a dead clam," the snipe said angrily.

"If it does not rain tomorrow or the next day, there will be a dead snipe, too," the clam answered back confidently.

"Tomorrow" did not arrive. A fisherman came by and caught both the clam and the snipe without any trouble.

Can you figure out, in this world, who is the clam, who is the snipe, and who is the fisherman, who gains the actual benefits?

The Tiger and the Cat

Zoologists tell us that the tiger and the cat belong to the same family, called felines. Both have almost the same physical constitution and similar outside form, except that one is big and heavy, and the other one is small and light. Most tigers are fierce and aggressive, while cats are supposed to be more domesticated and submissive. Therefore, the tiger and the cat do not get along very well in the world of animals.

But in China, people believe that, at the beginning, they were very intimate friends, and the cat was even much smarter than the tiger. The cat learned the physical skills quickly, and the tiger was always behind. Gradually, the tiger had to learn everything from the cat, and the cat was patient to teach the tiger. Day after day, month after month, finally, the tiger could also run, jump, roll, grasp, tear, and strike as well as the cat.

One day, the cat was taking a summer afternoon nap as the tiger sat nearby. Looking at the small cat, the tiger suddenly thought, why should he keep befriending such a small animal since he had already learned his skills from the cat? The evil tiger decided to kill the sleeping cat as a before-dinner snack. The tiger stood up and approached the cat viciously. Just at this moment, the cat woke up and opened his eyes. The cat realized what the tiger was trying to do and swiftly jumped on a nearby tree and climbed to the top branch.

The tiger thought he had learned everything from the cat. He never knew that the cat hid the tree climbing from him.

"I kept the last technique of the tree climbing from you just because I suspected you might be an ungrateful friend," the cat told the tiger, who watched under the tree helplessly.

Living in such a complicated, unpredictable society, who can guarantee that we shall never have a "tiger" friend? Maybe we individually should all hide a technique such as tree climbing in case we meet a sudden attack like the one the cat had. 🐾

The Eagle and the Donkey

It was a beautiful summer. The magical weather had turned the whole mountain green. The big animals, such as elephants and cows, were all taking naps after lunch under trees, while the small animals, such as rats and rabbits, were hiding themselves in their cool underground burrows.

The only one who was not afraid of being in the sunshine was a donkey, who was happily running up and down a muddy hill as a kind of self-amusing exercise.

In the sky, a hungry eagle flew over the mountain and looked for a small animal for his late lunch.

"Where are the small, tasty creatures?" The eagle kept asking himself this question for he had flown for several hours, but had still found nothing.

Finally, he saw the playful donkey. The eagle had eaten the meat of a donkey once. He remembered that it was almost as delicious as rabbit meat. But today this donkey was still alive.

The eagle stopped on the hill and watched the happy donkey coming up the hill again.

"Hello, my donkey friend," the eagle made a friendly start. "What are you busy doing?"

"It is fun to run up and down the hill," the donkey

answered. Then he asked, "Why are you not flying in the sky? I always thought it would be a lot of fun to fly."

"Yes, it is," the eagle said. Then the eagle had a wicked idea. He asked the donkey, "Do you want to learn to fly?"

"Me, fly?" The donkey stopped running, asking, "Are you crazy? Have you ever seen a flying donkey?"

"As far as I know, many kinds of animals can fly if they want to," said the eagle. "I did not know how to fly when I was young. My mother forced me to learn. Now, you see, I fly pleasantly all the time."

"You mean a donkey like me can also learn to fly? I don't believe it." Although the donkey said he did not believe it, the eagle said it so honestly that the donkey began to think maybe the eagle was right.

"Of course you can. It totally depends upon two important factors. First, you must have self-confidence. Second, you must have a good instructor like me."

"If I decide to learn to fly, would you teach me?" the donkey finally asked with interest.

"Sure, it is my pleasure," the eagle promised immediately.

The two animals soon made a deal. When the donkey finished his flying course from the eagle, the donkey would then teach the eagle how to run fast.

First, the eagle demonstrated a few basic actions before flying and asked the donkey to follow him.

The donkey did. But the eagle was not satisfied. The eagle kept demonstrating and kept correcting the donkey's imitations patiently. The donkey thought he was lucky to have such a good flying instructor.

"Whether I can fly or not now depends upon whether I have the self-confidence," the donkey thought. "If I can fly, that would clearly become the biggest news on the mountain."

The more the donkey thought, the more excited he became. He learned the new skills with more interest and confidence.

The eagle led the way to the brink of a precipice. The eagle showed the donkey how he jumped down from the precipice. The eagle flew up and landed on the brink again. He wanted his student donkey to follow his example.

Looking at the steep precipice, the donkey hesitated. He was afraid he could not fly back up and would fall to the bottom and die. He wanted the eagle to do one more demonstration, and the eagle did. After that, the eagle told his student about his own experience. When he was a child, he used to live on the top of a high tree. One day, his mother told him it was time for him to fly. He was afraid he might not be able to fly back up. He refused, just like the donkey. Suddenly the mother eagle pushed her son from the nest, and the young bird dropped toward the ground. In that moment, the young eagle learned to fly on his own. The teacher eagle told his student donkey that nothing could be achieved without courage.

Finally, the donkey made up his mind. He jumped off the cliff.

The teacher eagle immediately followed the student donkey.

A few minutes later, the hungry eagle happily filled his empty stomach with the fresh donkey meat at the bottom of the precipice.

After that, he comforted himself. "At least, I did not kill the donkey." 🐾

The Donkey and the Tiger

A Chinese man once rode a black donkey by an unknown small town at the foot of a high mountain.

The traveler was tired and hungry. After fastening the donkey to a post, he went into a restaurant to eat.

The people in the town had never seen a donkey before. Naturally, many people came over to take a closer look at the strange animal.

When a boy was using his hand to touch the donkey's neck, the animal suddenly brayed. The noise frightened the child, and he immediately ran away. After a while, when a woman walked by the donkey, the animal suddenly kicked out one of its back legs. Luckily the kicking did not hurt the woman, but it was strong enough to scare away all the people who gathered around the animal.

Seeing the quick disappearance of people, the donkey felt very proud of himself. He thought that he might be the most powerful animal in the world. As the donkey's master had not yet come back, the donkey got loose and sneaked out of town. He went up to the high mountain to satisfy his curiosity about the wild world.

In the woods, he soon met a tiger. The tiger had

never seen a donkey, either. He dared not approach the strange donkey and was ready to run away. Just at this moment, the donkey brayed. The noise frightened the tiger a little bit, so the tiger retreated a few steps and watched from a distance.

The donkey was happy. He thought the tiger must be a coward like the boy in town. He brayed again. This time, the tiger did not retreat. Instead, he walked a little closer to the donkey. Still the tiger dared not take any action. The donkey thought of the scared woman in the town, so he used one of his back legs to kick out. This action made the tiger afraid. The tiger hesitated about whether he should stay or run away from the unknown animal.

Meanwhile, the donkey thought that the tiger must be very afraid of his talents, so he kept braying and kicking. The more the donkey brayed and kicked, the less afraid the tiger became.

Finally, the tiger realized that aside from braying and kicking, the donkey had no other power. The tiger then pounced at the donkey and easily killed it. The poor donkey did not comprehend his own limitations and thus became the hungry tiger's supper.

This is a complicated society mixed with all kinds of people, including "tigers" and "donkeys." So, please hide some of your talents. Don't show off completely in front of strangers, and you'll avoid the destiny of the black donkey.

The Overconfident Mantis

A mantis is a tropical insect with two pairs of walking legs and a pair of huge forelimbs. A big mantis is often as long as five or six inches. It is commonly found in the grasses or fields in many parts of China during the summer.

In my homeland in eastern China, I used to play a game with the other children to see who could catch the biggest mantis. We had to be careful when we approached the mantises, as their two forelimbs extending like a pair of saws with their two sharp toothed edges could hurt our fingers.

According to the Chinese classic *Chuang-Tzu*, a certain mantis grew extraordinarily stout and robust. When he walked around in a backyard, brandishing his two powerful forelimbs, he could easily catch some smaller insects such as locusts, crickets, or bugs if he was hungry or mad that day. Since he was bigger and stronger and caught more smaller insects than his companions, he felt that he should be the leader of his kingdom.

His authority was one day challenged by another smaller, but strong, mantis. After bitter fighting, the big mantis defeated his challenger, who fled toward a road outside the backyard and disappeared. The victor went to the road, but he did not find the loser. He vented his anger on the small insects, killing one locust and two crickets. All the other small insects immediately escaped.

Suddenly, the bloodthirsty mantis stood bravely on the road himself. The joy of victory intoxicated him into thinking that he might be the most indomitable creature in the world. Soon, he heard a strange sound coming from the other way. It was a one-wheel wooden cart pushed by a man coming toward him on the road.

The mantis had never seen a wooden cart. He stood on the road brandishing his two powerful "saws" without retreat. He really believed that he could stop or frighten away the coming "monster," as he had defeated many enemies before.

In another minute, the wooden wheel rolled over the poor, self-important, ignorant mantis, crushing him without the cart driver's even knowing.

What the author of the classic wanted to tell us is that there are many "mantises" in our society, too. They are self-important and ignorant. They think they are superior to others. They overestimate their strength because they have never seen a "wooden cart."

A Chinese proverb says, "If you think you are the strongest, there is always somebody who is actually stronger than you; if you think your world is the biggest, there is always another world that is bigger than yours." 🐾

The Monkey and the Elephant

After a heavy lunch, a little monkey took a short nap between the branches on the top of a high tree. It was a hot, summer afternoon.

Suddenly, he was awakened by a desperate cry for help. Immediately, he found a stout mantis holding a delicate branch with his two sawlike forelimbs.

The insect was crying, "Help me, please," as a blackbird was about to kill him. Without hesitation, the monkey jumped over and scared away the attacker.

"Thank you so much for saving my life, Mr. Monkey," the mantis said, lowering his forelimbs. "When I discovered I was followed by a bird, I realized that if I moved, the bird would attack me immediately. If I stayed where I was, the bird would still attack me. If you had not come just in time, I would have been murdered already. I appreciate your help very much and will never forget your kindness."

"It was my pleasure," the monkey happily replied and then traveled to another tree.

"Saving a small creature's life is wonderful. I'll

keep doing things like that as much as possible in the future," the elated monkey said to himself as he leaped through abundant leaves and branches.

When he rested at a coarse branch, he heard another cry. Yes, it was more than one cry.

Following the direction of the sounds, the monkey soon found four small birds crying in a nest. They cried because they were desperately hungry. "I think I will die if Mom does not bring food back soon," one baby bird cried to the others, and all the others responded similarly.

At this moment, the mother bird flew back. Amid cheers, the large black bird comforted her babies. "Sorry, my dear children, I didn't bring you anything to eat this trip. A little while ago, I was almost sure to catch a fat mantis. If a naughty monkey had not interfered, that mantis would have made a good meal for my kids. Anyway, I'll keep looking for food for you."

The mother bird hastily kissed each of her children and flew away on her mission again, leaving the hungry little ones powerlessly crying.

Having quietly overheard the birds' conversation, the monkey was upset. He was totally confused. Did he do a good deed when he stopped a mother from bringing food to her hungry children? The monkey could not get the correct answer himself. He sorrowfully returned to the ground.

The monkey consulted an elephant on the serious question.

"You did nothing wrong," the authoritative

elephant told the monkey. "In this world, nobody can take care of everyone."

The elephant is right. Many times, we thought we did the perfect thing. Yet, it still produced an opposite "side effect." A Chinese philosopher said, "As long as we have done what we should, we cannot expect approval from everyone." 🐾

The Lion and the Squirrel

When a squirrel woke up from his summer afternoon nap, he was frightened to discover that he was clutched in the strong paw of a lion.

It was obvious the huge animal was going to enjoy the little creature as a small delicacy. The smart squirrel realized that trying to escape was almost impossible. He had to calm down and do something quickly in order to save his life.

"Mr. Lion," the squirrel said as calmly as he could, "you should not eat me without a fair contest. First, we must see whose power is stronger. Then we decide whether you eat me, or I eat you."

"A tiny animal like you dares to challenge a giant like me?" The lion laughed loudly. To show his generosity, the lion put down the squirrel and said, "Whatever the game is, I'll play it with you."

"Let us prove which one of us has more power." The squirrel stood up and showed the lion his small claws with confidence.

"Of course, I accept your suggestion." The lion suddenly smiled, as he had never met such a boastful self-murderer.

The squirrel asked, "What is the hardest thing in the jungle?" The squirrel himself then answered, "I would say the rocks."

"I agree," the lion replied.

"Let us both hit a rock with our bare fists. The one who can beat the rock until it bleeds should be the winner of the contest. Is it fair?" the squirrel asked.

"Absolutely fair," the lion agreed.

Then the lion started to hit a large rock in front of them with all the energy he had. A few minutes later, both of the lion's front paws were badly hurt, yet the rock was still in perfect shape.

"Nobody can make it bleed." The lion gave up and said to the squirrel, "Now it is your turn."

The small squirrel retreated a few steps, then suddenly ran to the rock. In a minute, the hard rock was indeed bleeding under the squirrel's claws.

"I cannot believe it," the lion yelled.

"But it is a fact," the squirrel answered.

Actually, the squirrel had hidden a small red grape in his claw while the lion was hitting the rock. All the squirrel had done was squeeze the grape against the rock to make it look as if the rock were bleeding.

"Let us try something different." The lion could not surrender easily, so he made another proposal. "Whoever can kill a smaller creature in one blow will be the winner this time."

To the lion's great surprise, the squirrel accepted the deal right away. Pointing to the ants running around the grasses, the squirrel said, "Mr. Lion, you kill the ants first."

When the mighty lion used his powerful paw to hit the running ants, he made a big hole in the ground, but all of the ants scampered away.

The small squirrel jumped over the grass, and, using his tiny claws, he easily killed a few ants right on the spot.

While the lion was still acting the fool, the squirrel had already jumped on a high tree and cheerfully told the lion, "The contest is over. Good-bye!"

A man's energy is limited, no matter how strong he is. A man's wisdom is unlimited, no matter how weak he is. A wise one knows how to get out of a crisis, while the unwise one will lose. 🐿

Kite Flying

Have you ever seen a kite fly? Did you fly kites when you were a child? Most children in China fly kites.

A kite has a light framework, made of thin bamboo branches, covered with paper. It is designed to climb and fly in a steady breeze at the end of a long string, while the person on the ground holds the other end of the string to control the kite. Most kites in China are made in the shapes of animals, especially birds. Kites have been popular in China since the sixth century, according to historical records.

Kite flying was one of my favorite childhood pastimes every spring in China. One of my senior cousins knew how to fly kites and always made kites for me. According to him, balancing the two wings was the key to make a kite stay in the sky.

I have lived in Wyoming for nineteen years, yet I seldom see the children here flying kites. A couple of years ago, I was very glad to see many children flying kites by Fisherman's Wharf in San Francisco. I found that there were hundreds of various kinds of kites for sale in the stores along the wharf. With the advancement of modern techniques, the kites were all made of plastic, instead of paper, such as the ones I used to play with, and they were much more colorfully painted.

When people hold the end of the string in their hand, they can control the kite's movement in the sky. Once the string is broken, the kite will suddenly fly higher and farther. But it will soon drop to the ground because of the loss of support of the string, according to my cousin's explanation.

There were once two kites flying in the sky. One had the shape of a horned owl, and the other had the shape of a wild goose.

It was a beautiful day. The white clouds amused themselves by floating around in the sky. The happy sun beamed with smiles toward everyone. The light spring breeze continued in one direction. The two kites flew side by side.

"Are you happy?" the horned owl asked the wild goose.

"Sure, I'm very happy," the goose answered.

"If I could get rid of the control of the boy who is holding the other end of my string on the ground, I could fly much higher and farther," said the horned owl. "Then, I would be much happier. I think I must gain my freedom and get rid of the boy's control." The owl was happy, yet he still complained.

Soon, the weather changed. The wind was blowing stronger and stronger. Seizing the opportunity, the horned owl finally broke the string and got rid of the boy's control. The owl indeed flew higher and farther. But, in another minute or so, he was blown over by the strong wind and dropped to the ground, broken into pieces. The other kite, the wild goose, his former companion, controlled by the boy on the ground, was still flying in the sky.

Freedom is the target every person pursues. But freedom does not mean that people can do whatever they want, regardless of the rules. It must be part of a reasonable political system. People have freedom. The government must have laws to restrict and support the freedom. That is the way a well-organized society is supposed to be. Without solid cooperation, there is often big chaos, such as what happened to the horned owl kite. 🦌

The Crocodile and the Monkey

A carefree monkey lived in a jungle. He was honest and sincere to others and had many friends. He was a smart animal, never had any evil thoughts, and always trusted his friends.

One late afternoon, after jumping around in the trees all day, he went to a river to wash his dirty hands. A crocodile swam over. The monkey had no friends in the water, so he said "Hello" to the crocodile.

The crocodile was a wicked animal. He was hungry, and he had heard that a monkey's liver was delicious. The crocodile approached the monkey and asked, "My dear friend monkey, have you ever traveled to the other side of the river?"

When the monkey replied that he had not, the crocodile said, "I just came over from the other shore. There are many more large delicious peaches over there than on this side of the river."

"But I don't know how to swim." The monkey was interested and had to tell the truth.

Then the crocodile offered that the monkey could stand on his back, and he would take the monkey across the river. It sounded like a good idea. The monkey jumped on the crocodile's back without hesitation.

In the middle of the river, the crocodile began to sink into the water, which frightened the monkey.

"Brother Crocodile," the monkey begged, "please don't keep sinking. I know nothing about swimming."

"I know you don't swim," the crocodile answered loudly with a vicious laugh. "I want to drown you so I'll have delicious monkey liver as my supper."

At this moment, the monkey realized that the whole thing was a trick. There were no larger peaches on the other shore. He himself was in immediate danger. But the monkey was smart. He calmed down immediately and replied, "Brother Crocodile, why didn't you say so earlier? I forgot to bring my liver with me. I cleaned it this morning and hung it up on the branch of a tall tree. Let's go back to the shore, and I'll give it to you right away."

The crocodile was disappointed, but in order to have delicious monkey liver for dinner, he took the monkey back to the shore and followed the monkey to a tall tree. While the crocodile was watching the monkey jump up on the tree, the careless crocodile did not notice a trap made by a hunter to catch animals by the tree.

The crocodile accidentally fell into the deep hole. He yelled for help. The monkey jumped back to the edge of the trap and said, "Listen, crocodile, I treated you as a sincere friend. But you are not. You are but a stupid reptile. Have you ever seen any animal take out his liver for cleaning? I am sorry. I cannot help you. The hunter will come and get your skin to sell. Maybe you deserve it. Good-bye." 🐾

A Fox with Tiger's Power

A hungry tiger caught a fox and planned to eat the fox as a delicious dinner.

The crafty fox pretended that he was not frightened at all. He said to the tiger seriously, "Wait a minute, tiger. You cannot eat me or even hurt me a little bit, because I am sent by Heaven as the king of the woods. All animals in the woods are supposed to respect me and hide immediately when they see me."

"I never heard of it," said the tiger. Yet, the tiger still set the fox down.

"It is easy to prove what I have just told you," the fox suggested confidently. "Follow me, tiger. Let us go back to the woods together."

The tiger was suspicious. He followed the fox closely for he was afraid the fox might escape. Meanwhile, the tiger told himself, "I am going to chew every bone of you if you are telling me a lie."

But, to the great surprise of the tiger, all the small animals really ran away as soon as they saw the small fox together with a strong fierce tiger.

A fact was a fact. The tiger had to believe what he had seen.

The tiger suddenly changed his attitude and said

to the conceited fox respectfully, "I am awfully sorry, Your Highness. You are absolutely right."

The tiger bowed off, and the fox climbed a tall tree to have a relaxing nap, where the tiger and other strong fierce animals could not reach him.

The story is a famous Chinese fable. In China, if we meet someone who is very hard to deal with, because of his powerful family background, we call the person "a fox with tiger's power." 🐾

The Monk and the Wolf

A hunter discovered a wolf and drew his bow to shoot it. He shot the wolf, but the wolf ran away and soon disappeared.

On the other side of the mountain curve, an old Chinese Buddhist monk was carrying a large bag of crops, walking slowly by himself. The injured wolf suddenly showed up asking for help.

"My dear, kind monk," the wolf knelt down in front of the monk and begged, "you always have mercy on animals. I need your help very badly. A hunter just hurt me, and he is chasing me. If you save my life, I will never forget your kindness and will repay your favor with all I can."

The monk immediately emptied his bag and let the wolf hide in it. In a few minutes, the hunter arrived and asked the monk if he had seen an injured wolf. The monk answered, "No," and the hunter left.

The monk opened the bag and told the wolf to come out. The monk was indeed a very kind person. He also pulled out the arrow that had been stabbed into the wolf's back.

The wolf stood up and looked around. He found that there was nobody nearby except the old monk and himself. He said to the monk, "Thank you for your help. You'll have to help me again. I have not eaten for a whole day and am awfully hungry. I must eat you, or I'll starve to death."

"How can you repay my kindness like this?" This monk could not believe it. He argued with the wolf, "You cannot do that."

"You should not have saved me, but it is too late now. You know I am a wolf. I am very hungry. I am injured. I cannot find any better food to eat. I'll have to eat you right now." Then the wolf tried to attack the monk.

"Wait a minute." The monk retreated and begged, "Let us find another person to judge. If the third party agrees with you, I will let you eat me without complaint."

The wolf agreed to the suggestion, as he thought the monk would not run away. They both went back to the road. Pretty soon, they met a politician. The monk told the politician the whole story and asked for a fair judgment.

The crafty wolf said to the politician, "When the monk put me in the bag, he intentionally closed the bag very tight. I almost died from lack of air. He wants to murder me. So I must eat him."

The monk immediately explained that he had to close the bag very tightly. Otherwise, the hunter would have detected the trick.

It seemed both sides were trying to win over the politician.

"I am a politician. I believe only what I have

seen. I cannot make a judgment unless the wolf goes back into the monk's bag and lets the monk close the bag again. Then I shall decide if the monk did something wrong before."

It was a deal. Both the plaintiff and the defendant agreed.

The wolf went back into the bag, and the monk closed the bag tightly just as he had done before. The politician further used a strong rope to bind the bag's opening to make sure the wolf would not come out again.

The politician then declared, "As a judge, I sentence that the wolf should receive the death penalty for his evil thought and action."

Before the wolf had a chance to argue, the politician judge pulled out his knife and did the execution right on the spot.

We, as human beings, should sympathize with the weak and small and give them all the help we can. The Buddhist monk did nothing wrong. But sometimes religion can solve only part of the problem. We must also have a good political system to protect the people from the "wolves" in our society. ❦

Mr. Fool Wants
to Move the Mountain

In the province of Shan-Hsi, China, there once lived an old man known as Mr. Fool. Mr. Fool and his family had lived between a high mountain and the sea for a great number of generations. His home was built by the foot of the mountain called Tai-hang.

On the other side of the mountain, there were towns and cities that connected with other parts of the nation, but there was no town, not even a small one, on the same side by Mr. Fool's home. Therefore, Mr. Fool and his family had to go around the high mountain every time they needed to go shopping.

It was very inconvenient, but the Fool family had no desire to move to the other side of the mountain. They enjoyed living at the place where their ancestors had built and lived. Yet, the inconvenience remained whenever they went to town.

Finally, Mr. Fool made a decision. He called a family meeting and suggested moving the mountain to the sea. After a serious discussion, the whole family gave him solid agreement and support.

One fine day, Mr. Fool and his children and grandchildren formally started the moving.

In ancient China, there was no machinery. The Fool family had to use their bare hands with the help of simple tools to begin the huge mountain-moving project. Such a tremendous plan attracted people from the other side of the mountain. Those who came to see it thought Mr. Fool was crazy.

"Mr. Fool," an outspoken observer warned, "you must realize that you are more than eighty years old. You won't have many more years to live. Even if you were a young man, with the limited man-power of your family, how could you expect to move such a high mountain to the faraway sea?"

"You might be right," Mr. Fool answered honestly. "In fact, I do not expect to completely move away the mountain during my lifetime. All I am doing is getting a good start. My children and my grandchildren will take over the job after my death. After their death, their children and grandchildren will continue the moving, and so will their offspring. Since the mountain does not grow any more, one of these days, it will be completely moved to the sea."

Then he led his family work force to the project again, ignoring laughs and criticism.

What a firm resolution it was! This obstinate res-olution made the gods of mountain and sea worry. They were afraid that the beautiful shapes of moun-tain and sea would eventually be destroyed by the Fool family. After an urgent joint conference, the two deities hastily reported the event to the superior universal ruler. The ruler immediately used his mar-velous power to move the mountain to the other side of Mr. Fool's home that same night.

From the next day on, the Fool family did not ever again have to go around the mountain when they went to town to go shopping.

Of course, the story is but a Chinese myth. Today, we take a jet and travel around the world within a few days. We talk with other people by overseas long-distance telephone. We sit at home watching television and know immediately what is going on around the world.

When the inventors of those modern conveniences had their "crazy" ideas in the beginning, they were also laughed at by others. People said, too, they were planning to move a "high mountain to the sea."

An old Chinese proverb says that because previous generations planted trees for us, we are able to enjoy the pleasant shade under leaves and branches. If nobody wants to do the "planting," how can we enjoy the jet, the telephone, and the television? Maybe we all need the foolish spirit of Mr. Fool to carry on our work.

The Ghost of Poverty

It is said that after death, people become ghosts.

It is further said that there are many kinds of ghosts, and one of them is called the ghost of poverty. According to old Chinese books, once a ghost of poverty moved into a house, the family would lose fortune and become poor people. Therefore, many poor folks in ancient China tried hard to drive out the ghost of poverty.

One Chinese man thought that the reason he was so poor was that the ghost of poverty must have arrived in his home. Although he used every way to expel the ghost, he was still in great financial straits. Finally, he gave up trying. He closed the door and murmured by himself in a dark corner where he believed the ghost of poverty was hiding.

He said to the ghost, in a very firm and serious manner, that he was going to starve himself to death. After death, he would become a ghost, too. Thus he could actually meet the ghost of poverty.

He swore that he would fight to the death with the ghost of poverty, which had made him live in this miserable situation. He warned that he would not let the ghost easily escape, once he himself became a ghost. If the ghost of poverty was afraid of the deadly fight, he should leave the house within three days, before the master of the house became a ghost, too.

Then, the man lay on the bed, without eating or drinking or doing anything. He was waiting for death.

At the end of three days, the man opened his eyes and saw a small bag of pennies left at the corner of his room. It meant that the ghost of poverty did not want to have the deadly fight and had sneaked out of the house. The ghost had surrendered.

The man picked up the moneybag. He resumed his eating habits. By the next day, his fate indeed changed. He worked hard, and he made much money. Eventually he became a rich person.

Of course, poverty is not a crime. We do not have to feel ashamed. Yet we must face the tight corner all the time. If we want to extricate ourselves from financial straits, we have to stand up and be ready to fight with the ghost of poverty. With a solid plan and firm determination, every poor person can get rid of poverty. We do not want to live with such a ghost. We can overcome distress by counting on ourselves. ❦

How to Counteract Resentment

A Chinese doctor invented a medicine that, according to the doctor, could make a person easily win and keep solid friendship, even with those who used to dislike him.

Since the medicine had no side effects, and the price was so reasonable that every person could afford it, almost everyone in town took the medicine. It was certainly a wonderful medicine. Consequently, no argument or fight had happened in town since the medicine was introduced. The crime rate suddenly dropped to almost zero, and the whole town was like a big happy family. People cared about each other as if they were brothers and sisters.

One day, a stranger came to the town. He had heard of the wonderful medicine. He asked the manager of a restaurant to resell some of the medicine to him after he had dinner at the café. He took it and left town in a hurry.

A week later, the same man came back to the town. He went to see the doctor who invented the medicine. "Doctor," the stranger said, "every person in town told me about your wonderful medicine.

I bought some and took it a week ago. It does not work well at all. In the last week, I had two fights with my wife and one big argument with my business friend. They would not agree with me, and I could not agree with them, either."

"When you bought the medicine from the restaurant manager," the doctor asked, "did he tell you how to take it?"

"I was too busy to ask for details. I just took it with water that day. What do you mean, 'How to take it'?" The stranger was confused.

The doctor then explained that the secret of taking the medicine was the attitude of the person taking it. The person must sincerely think about and genuinely act out how to forgive. Otherwise, the medicine would not work.

Another week passed, and the same man reappeared in the doctor's office. He was very happy to tell the doctor that the medicine had really worked this time.

No one is perfect. Every person makes mistakes. As long as one did not purposely intend to make a mistake, or if he has bitterly paid for the mistakes and now expresses how sorry he is, why not forgive him and give him a chance to start again as a new man?

The old Buddhist monks always urge people to replace resentment with favor. They believe that this is the only way to melt away hatred and feud. It is this principle, not the medicine itself, which made Germany, Italy, and Japan become friends again with the old Allied powers.

Therefore, as much as you can, please forgive the mistakes somebody might have done concerning you. Who knows, maybe one of these days, somebody will do the same favor for you, too, when you happen to make a mistake. 🌑

Don't Wait for the Rabbit

An Associated Press news report said that a woman jogging along a roadway near Great Falls, Montana, happened to find a gold-colored stone. She took the bright stone to a jewelry shop wanting to set it in a ring. She was overjoyed to be told that it was the first fourteen-carat uncut diamond ever found in the United States.

The newspaper did not report whether the woman kept jogging along the same roadway or how many other joggers joined her by the road.

In ancient China, a similar incident happened.

A Chinese farmer lived in a place called Sung. He got up every morning and went to the field to work. When the sun began to set, he returned home. In those days, there was no farm machinery. A farmer had only limited tools, with the help of a cow or horse sometime, to do all the necessary work. If the farmer worked diligently, he could make a simple living.

Life was dull until one day. While he was plowing the field, he suddenly saw a rabbit dashing toward a big tree by the roadside not too far from him. Because of running too fast or perhaps being frightened, the poor animal did not escape the tree. He hit the strong trunk and died right on the spot. Soon, the farmer saw a wild dog running by. The rabbit had probably been pursued by the dog, resulting in this tragic accident.

The farmer swiftly went over to the tree and picked up the dead rabbit. He took it home and asked his wife to cook it. They had delicious rabbit stew that evening. The next day, the farmer sold the rabbit's fur in town and also made a small profit.

This kind of good luck certainly did not happen very often. It was very unusual. But, from that time on, the foolish farmer quit his usual daily work. He still came to the land, but did nothing. He would sit by the tree where he had found the dead rabbit. He was waiting for another good-luck event. Day after day, week after week, the farmer wasted his time in this most unpractical dream, and no second rabbit ever hit the tree.

In China, if a person had good luck in the past and discontinues working as hard as he is supposed to, but dreams of having the same good luck again, the person will be called "a farmer waiting for a rabbit."

Although some events of life may be discouraging, we should not count on repeat good luck and slow down the hard work we are doing. The rabbit may hit the tree again. We may find another uncut diamond by the roadway. But no one can be sure when. We must forget the dead animal and keep plowing the field with our own hands. 🍂

The Scholar and the King

A private firm in Taiwan once conducted an opinion poll among high school students: which kind of person would they want to be like when they grow up, Wang Yang-ching or Wu Ta-yu?

Wang was a high-school dropout, but supposedly the richest person in Taiwan. He owns many successful enterprises throughout the world. Dr. Wu was the president of Academia Sinica, the highest academic research institute in Taiwan. He was supposed to be the most knowledgeable person in that country.

The newspaper said the choice in the polls was Dr. Wu.

In early China, people respected the emperor or king and the scholars most. Almost every emperor respected scholars. If a certain emperor did not, that ruler would not be praised in the history. If a scholar flattered the emperor, that scholar would not be praised, either.

About 2,300 years ago, the king of Chi (a kingdom of China) received a very well-known scholar, Yan Chu. Because the two persons sat at a distance, the king could not hear Yan very well. So the king told Yan, "Come over and sit a little bit closer to me."

Yan heard the king's order, yet he did not move. Instead, he answered the king, "Your Majesty, you come over and sit a little bit closer to me."

Yan's rude reply made both the king and his senior officials angry. Every person blamed Yan. One top official loudly asked Yan, "Who is more glorious, the king or the scholar? And who should listen to whom?"

Yan slowly stood up, but he still did not move closer. He replied to the official seriously, "Before answering your questions, let me tell you the reason I did not move to the king and asked the king to move to me.

"If I humbly moved my chair toward the king, the people of the whole nation of Chi would say that I was but an ordinary man who, like all of the officials, liked to flatter the king.

"If the king moved his chair toward me, the people of the whole nation would all praise the king, who held the most power, but respected the knowledge of a scholar.

"Do you want our king to be highly praised by all the people, or do you want our king not to be praised at all?"

The answer made the king of Chi suddenly change his attitude. The king immediately moved his chair closer to the well-known scholar, Yan Chu.

When other scholars heard the story, they all voluntarily came to the palace offering their advice to the king. The kingdom of Chi became a highly civilized nation.

Money, power, and knowledge are probably the three most important things people all over the world would like to pursue. Money and power can help people attain what they want, but what they get will not last forever. Knowledge is different. Without knowledge, time will still move on, but we shall stay where we are without further advancement.

I am glad that the Taiwanese students made the right choice when they selected their idol in life. ❦

Self-Confidence
and Humility

Tso Chung-tang was a famous Chinese general in the Ching dynasty about 120 years ago.

Tso was a success, yet he was not humble, especially when he played Wei-chi, a kind of complicated Oriental chess, very popular in China and Japan. For years, he was the champion of Wei-chi in the Chinese army.

One evening, before a big battle the next day, Tso and his bodyguards took a walk after supper. He happened to see a small wooden sign hanging on the door of a store. It read: "The World's Number One Wei-chi Player."

General Tso was startled. He ordered one of his guards to go inside the store and ask who was the number one chess player. General Tso Chung-tang wanted to challenge the number one player to three games of Wei-chi. An old man came out and invited Tso and his men into the store.

The old man accepted the general's challenge. They had three games. It turned out that General Tso was still the champion. He won every game. He left the store with self-confidence as usual. He led his troops to the battle the next morning, and he won the battle.

Upon his happy return to the city, Tso revisited the old man. They played chess again. To his great surprise and dismay, Tso lost all the games, one after the other. For the whole afternoon, he did not win one game. Upon the repeated request of Tso, the old man smiled and told the general the true story. "The first time we played the game, I realized that you were leading the troops to war the next day. I was afraid that if you lost the game, it might affect your self-confidence, which is very important in battle. Therefore, I purposely let you win every game. Now, you have won the battle, so we can play the game fairly."

General Tso stood up immediately and bowed to the old man in appreciation for what he had received from the old man. For the rest of General Tso's life, he was humble toward everyone.

Self-confidence is necessary for every successful person. After that, you must be humble, like General Tso, in order to keep your good reputation. 🍂

Keeping a Promise

A promise means that you told someone that you would do something. If you fail to do it, it could be interpreted that you have told a lie or deceived somebody.

People make promises lots of times, and lots of people never keep their promises.

When we train young children not to tell a lie, one of the best methods is to remind them to carry out their promises. If people always carry out what they have promised, they should be a success. This training should start from childhood.

Tseng-tzu was one of Confucius's seventy-two outstanding students. One day, Tseng-tzu's wife was preparing to do some shopping. Their young son asked to go with her. She did not want the boy to go with her shopping, so she tricked him. "Stay home with daddy. I'll be back very soon. We'll kill our pig, and I'll cook you a very good pork dinner tonight," she said.

After shopping, she came home and was surprised to find her husband, Tseng-tzu, catching the pig and preparing to kill it.

"What are you doing with our only pig which is still too young to be killed?" Obviously, she had forgotten what she had promised her son before her shopping trip.

"I am going to kill the pig and let you cook a pork dinner tonight, as you promised our son," Tseng-tzu answered unhappily, but firmly.

"What I promised our son was but a trick, because I did not want to take him with me while I was shopping," Tseng-tzu's wife replied.

Tseng-tzu stood up and told his wife very seriously, "Of course, I did not want to kill our young pig today. All I am doing is carrying out your promise. Our son is a child. The words and actions of parents are the model for the child. If we do not keep our promise to him, how can we expect our child to carry out his promises when he grows up?"

Tseng-tzu did kill their young pig, and his wife did cook a pork dinner for the family that night. The story of Tseng-tzu and his pig has since been told by generation after generation in the history of China. 🍂

Leaders Must Be Open

Not many people like to be criticized for the mistakes they make. The persons who have the most power are often the ones who dislike criticism most. Consequently, in the old days, no Chinese official dared to blame their emperor even if the emperor made a big mistake.

There was an exception. The person was Tang Tai-tsung of the seventh century, the founder/emperor of the Chinese Tang dynasty.

Wei Cheng was one of Emperor Tang's top officials. He often criticized the emperor's personal acts, besides the official affairs, and he sometimes even made the criticism in front of many other officials. According to Wei Cheng, the emperor should be the model for his officials, and the officials should be the models for the common people. Then, the nation would be prosperous and in good order.

One day, Wei was called to the emperor's office to discuss an important issue. When Wei stepped into the office, he noticed that the emperor was playing with a quail. Many rich Chinese enjoyed these small birds as pets at home in those days. The emperor, however, was playing with the bird at the office on office time. The emperor hid the bird in his pocket immediately, in order to avoid Wei's criticism. In fact, Wei had already noticed the hiding, so he purposely stayed at the emperor's office much longer than expected, discussing many subjects with the emperor. After Wei left, Emperor Tang was sad to discover that his favorite quail had died in his pocket due to lack of air.

Tang Tai-tsung finally lost his patience with Wei this time. He left his office and angrily told his queen that he would kill Wei sooner or later because of Wei's continuous, direct, sharp criticism of his mistakes.

The queen returned to her room and soon came out in her most official full dress. She bowed to the emperor and said, "Congratulations, Your Majesty."

"For what?" Emperor Tang was confused.

"I have been told," the queen said, "if an emperor is virtuous and sagacious enough, his top officials would dare criticize the emperor's mistakes without fear of being punished. Wei Cheng keeps correcting your mistakes. It means that Your Majesty must be the most virtuous and sagacious emperor."

Emperor Tang was suddenly ashamed of his thought of killing Wei. Instead, he ordered a big promotion of Wei Cheng and asked all the other top officials to take Wei's honesty and loyalty as a good example. He told his officials that Wei was like his "mirror." Facing Wei every day was like looking into a mirror to check his thoughts and actions.

The time of Tang Tai-tsung's administration was one of the most prosperous periods in Chinese history. Emperor Tang's willingness to accept his official's criticism was probably one of the reasons for the prosperity.

Yen Ying, a Smart Official

In early China, under monarchism, a king or a ruler had much more absolute power than a political leader in today's democratic government. Chi was a kingdom in China more than 2,600 years ago. It was ruled by a duke.

One day, the duke of Chi discovered that his favorite bird had flown away. In a wild fury, he ordered the immediate execution of the low official who was in charge of the palace birds.

Yen Ying, a top official, heard of this order and begged to postpone the execution. Yen asked the duke if he could first tell the low official how serious that mistake was before the execution.

As the duke agreed, Yen loudly scolded the poor frightened man in front of the angry duke. "You are punished to death because of the following charges:

"Number one, you were careless in letting our duke's favorite bird fly away.

"Number two, you are making our virtuous duke kill a person because of a small animal.

"Number three, your death will make all the other kingdoms know that the duke of Chi lost a loyal official because of a bird."

When Yen Ying had barely finished his last sentence, the smart duke stood up and hastily stopped him. He announced, "I understand what you mean. Without your advice, I almost made a serious mistake. The man is excused."

Under the leadership of the duke and his top helper, Yen Ying, the kingdom of Chi became a prosperous nation. 🐦

Never Forget
a Benefit Conferred

One day, a middle-aged woman in San Francisco unexpectedly received a check for $20,000. It was from a recently deceased old man whom she probably met once when she was a small child.

The happy surprise made her cry for quite a while, for the money came at the perfect time and she was in urgent need of financial help.

Back in 1944, the woman's parents once offered warm hospitality to a few servicemen who were being shipped out to the South Pacific along with her two elder brothers in the navy. Ever since then, one of the servicemen had kept in touch with this kind host family through Christmas cards, until both of her parents passed away.

A few months ago, the former serviceman, then a successful California businessman, died of cancer. Before death, he remembered the warm hospitality he had once received from the kind couple. He left $20,000 in his will to their surviving children. The woman was her parents' youngest child and only heir, so the money came to her.

A similar story happened in China about 2,200

years ago. A discouraged young man named Huan Hsin was fishing by the river of Husi in Kiang-su province. He had not eaten anything for almost two days and hoped to catch some fish for a meal. But it seemed that he did not have any luck.

Meanwhile, not far away, an old laundrywoman was washing clothes by the river. When she realized his situation, she immediately offered him her own simple lunch. The young man finished the cold meal quickly and said good-bye to the old woman. Later, he went into the army. It was in the last years of the Chin dynasty. The huge empire was falling, and all China was in revolt.

Huan Hsin was a military genius. He helped the rebellious leader Liu Pang in defeating all the other ambitious rebelling groups. When Liu became the founding emperor of the 400-year-old Han dynasty, Huan was appointed a minister of merits. One day, after Huan had finished a luxurious state dinner with the emperor and many other dignitaries, he suddenly remembered the simple box lunch offered to him by an old laundrywoman while he was starving by the river. He ordered his soldiers to locate the kind old lady. When they found her, he personally presented her with a gift of many pounds of gold, which was so unexpected by the poor old lady. Thus, she had a very comfortable life in her last years.

An earnest Chinese Confucian scholar taught his offspring many moral laws. Among them, there were two clauses: "Have no recollection of favors given; never forget a benefit conferred."

This Oriental philosophy applies to both the Chinese general Huan Hsin and the American businessman in California. No matter where, in the East or the West, no matter when, a couple of thousand years ago, or in the late twentieth century, love is spread through appreciation and remembering all the time. 🍎

Twin Goddesses of Fortune and Misery

One day, a dignified lady in full splendid dress visited a home. She told the host that she was the goddess of fortune. She would bring fortune to the family she visited. The whole family warmly welcomed the guest. They treated the goddess-visitor with the best wine and food, trying every way they could to keep the guest with them as long as possible.

Before the end of the day, somebody else knocked upon the door. The hostess went to open it, and another woman walked in. She wore tattered clothes and looked like a beggar. She introduced herself as the goddess of misery.

When the family tried to reject the unwelcome visitor, she told them that she and the goddess of fortune were twin sisters. She explained the rules of heaven ordained that each of the two sisters could not stay at one home too long. If one showed up, the other must leave. The two sisters were not allowed to stay at one place at the same time.

While the family was speaking to the goddess of misery, the goddess of fortune suddenly disappeared. The incident made the whole family angry.

They commanded the goddess of misery to leave. But, no matter how hard the family tried, they could not expel the goddess of misery.

Finally, the family gave in. They compromised with the unwelcome visitor and figured out a method so they could live together under the same roof. Every member of the family had to learn how to live together with the goddess of misery. It was tough, but they learned.

On the third day, when the goddess of fortune returned to the house, her sister, the goddess of misery, immediately went away. The family became happy again.

In the world of human beings, joy and suffering are inseparable. Every person has both joy and suffering. Some people have more suffering than joy. Some have more joy than suffering. But, no one has joy or suffering all the time.

As good times do not last forever, a person must appreciate the "effort" the goddess of fortune brings. Meanwhile, the person must also learn how to meet the challenges of the difficulties presented by the goddess of misery.

When dark clouds gather in the sky, we survive and wait. We know that a clear day will soon return.

Another Secret of Success

I had never seen a faucet until 1945 when I was thirteen years old and my family moved to the capital of our province, after World War II ended.

Before 1945, we had all lived on a farm for generation after generation, far away from the city. There was no "automatic water" from the faucet in those days in the Chinese country.

Our family owned a large farm, and we had a large family that consisted of about thirty members in four generations, plus more than twenty servants, and we all lived together "under one roof."

One of our male servants' jobs was to carry the water daily from a nearby pond to the four huge vats in the yard for our fifty people. Half a century later, I still remember the name of our water carrier, Wu Shan. I remember how he carried water. He balanced a flat bamboo pole across his shoulders, with a wooden bucket full of water hanging from each end of the pole.

Is it easy to carry water?

A poor young fellow in China once asked an old, rich, successful man the secret of success. The old man told the young fellow, "If you can fill up my water vat, you will get the secret."

"It is an easy job for me," the young man said to himself. He happily accepted the two wooden buckets and a flat bamboo pole from the old man. He immediately started the job of carrying water to the old man's water vat.

As the sun set behind a mountain, the young man had almost filled up half the vat. "I will definitely make it tomorrow," he thought and returned home. But the next morning, when he came back to work, he was surprised to find that there was no water at all in the vat.

Soon, he found several holes in the bottom of the vat. He came to the old man and asked for another vat with no holes. The old man showed him another vat, gave him another two buckets, and took back the original two. The two new buckets were badly broken. By the time he carried the water to the vat, most of the water had already leaked out. He had no choice but to pour the small amount of water into the vat. Although it was a whole day's supply of water, he filled up less than one-twentieth of the huge vat.

The young man was discouraged and wanted to give up. But when he thought about getting the secret of being rich, he exerted himself and went back to the pond again the next day. Day after day, he continued his work. He lost track of how many trips he had made from the pond to the vat. Finally, the huge vat was full of water on the twenty-sixth day. The poor young man appeared in front of the rich, old man again proudly asking for the secret of success.

"My dear boy," the rich old man smiled as he told the young man, "I am not telling you a lie. There is actually no secret of success. If you have to name one, that would be perseverance. If you keep doing anything like the way you carried water, I am sure you will be successful and rich." 🍂

Are You a General
or a Soldier?

A young friend asked me one day, "When you take your girlfriend to a bar, and your girlfriend is insulted by other guys, what should you do?"

I hesitated for a moment, as I had never been in a situation like that.

The young friend then told me about his fight last weekend, resulting in a black eye and a few other bruises on his face and arms. He said that he fought bravely against two heavy, muscular men.

I comforted him by saying that if the policemen had not come in time, or if the two guys had had some kind of weapon, the result could have been much worse. I then told him the following Chinese story.

Huan Hsin was probably the most capable general in the Chinese Han dynasty (206 b.c. to a.d. 220). Without General Huan Hsin, there would have been no 400-year Han dynasty in Chinese history.

When Huan Hsin was a young man, he was very ambitious. Like many other young fellows, Huan Hsin often girded a sword when he went out. One day, he was confronted by two rascals who were much stronger than he. They challenged Huan to a duel if he thought he was brave enough; otherwise, they wanted Huan to take off his sword and crawl between the legs of one of the two rascals.

Since Huan Hsin was a very ambitious man, he did not want to be killed or badly injured by the two rough, mean strangers. Without much consideration, Huan took off his sword and did what he had been ordered to do, despite the laughter of bystanders.

Later on, Huan Hsin became the commander in chief of Han's army of millions of soldiers. He helped Emperor Liu Pang defeat all enemies and establish the powerful four-century-old Han dynasty.

For 2,000 years, none of the Chinese historians have ever thought that General Huan's crawling between a rascal's legs was a contemptible event. In China, if a situation like this happened to a young man, people would always encourage the young man to avoid taking meaningless action, as did General Huan Hsin, in order not to ruin the big plan in the future.

My young friend listened to my story and left without saying much. I could tell from his face that he did not want to argue with me about the aged Chinese philosophy, as this is the United States of America, and we are in the twentieth century.

Of course, it is not easy to digest an insult. An old Chinese proverb says, "Restraining momentary anger may save you a hundred years of sorrow." The former "hero" who sits in jail facing countless days ahead should realize the meaning of this old Chinese philosophy.

A master of the Chinese martial art kung fu never teaches a student until the teacher is sure that the student knows how to endure contempt.

There is a big difference between forbearance and cowardice. The former looks forward to a bright future, while the latter sees only the present. The person who can forbear to hit back may become a general, and the person who is afraid of being called a coward may be only a brave soldier.

Furthermore, if you cannot digest an insult, and you do not want to have meaningless fighting, you will have to learn how to develop self-esteem. A famous Chinese philosopher warned, "Meat decays first; maggots come later." You must do your best not to let the meat decay; then the maggots will not come to you. ❧

A Snake Has No Feet

A Chinese art teacher took his students out for a picnic in the woods. He wanted to take advantage of the moment to teach young fellows how to do practical, lifelike portrayals.

It was a fine summer morning. They did lots of paintings and enjoyed a good meal.

After eating, the teacher found there was still one small bottle of wine left. A snake happened to appear close by. The teacher amusingly suggested, "Whoever finishes painting the snake first wins the wine."

"It is a deal!" one tall student quickly answered. He was a fast painter and one of the top students in the class.

Since it was a fair contest, the rest of the students joyfully agreed. Within ten minutes, the student who agreed first, finished the drawing. It was a vivid rattlesnake, with its head fearlessly lifted and the tongue sharply extended, crawling on a big rock. He showed the painting to the teacher, who nodded in praise.

The student seemed sure of winning the contest. It was actually an honor to win, not just to receive the small bottle of wine.

While all the other students were working, the apparent winner had nothing to do. He stood up and walked a few steps, then sat down. Still no one else finished. He picked up his painting again and added a few lines on the rock. Jokingly, he even put four feet under the snake's abdomen to make the snake "walk."

The teacher finally gathered all the students' works and made his decision. Much to his disappointment, the fast painter, the top student who had finished the snake drawing first, was not the winner. He had done an excellent job, and he had finished it before all the others. But he failed. The reason he did not win the wine, according to the teacher's judgment, was his last-minute addition. A snake has no feet. He had not drawn a snake, but a creature of his own wild imagination.

In China, for tens of hundreds of years, if a person did something extra, and the additional job spoiled the whole project, people would say he was "adding feet to a snake." In order to win fairly in today's competitive society, we must work hard and do the job just right. Extra work is acceptable, but not always appreciated. Sometimes it can even bring a negative impact. When we go to a circus and enjoy the aerial acrobatics, we admit that none of them "add a foot to the snake" while they are flying in the air. 🐦

Don't Forget Who You Are

Do you know who you are? I am pretty sure you do. But a Chinese woman who got off a train at a station in northern Taiwan kept asking people who she was, according to a Chinese newspaper published in California.

She told the police officer that after she woke up from a nap on the train, she suddenly forgot who she was, where she came from, and where she was going. She asked for help.

From her manner of talking, she did not appear to be a psychiatric patient. With the help of the police department, her husband was found and came to pick her up. The man told police officers that his wife had spells of amnesia, caused by an automobile accident, and the medical doctors could not find a cure. Her amnesia came and went.

Menicius (372-289 B.C.) was a sincere adherent of Confucianism. He believed that every person's nature was good by birth. By practice, people got to be far apart. Some were still good people as they followed the rules of society and always stayed with nice fellows, while some would turn out to be bad persons because they went with evildoers all the time. The circumstance, the external world, made a person become a merciless bandit. When a bandit woke up and realized his mistakes, his goodness would return. He would then be a nice man again.

Unfortunately, many evildoers never wake up. In China, when the old generations find that their younger ones are likely moving toward evil ways, they would often remind the youngsters, "Don't forget who you are." It means that the young fellows were good persons in the beginning, and they must not forget their original nature.

To check whether he had done anything wrong, Confucius said that he examined himself three times a day. It is not easy for everyone to follow this practice. I do like to examine myself once in a while, however, closing the door of my private den, sitting by the window in solitude. I ask myself who I am and what I have been doing. We might not have amnesia like the Chinese woman in Taiwan, but we still might get lost in the vast "external world" if we never give ourselves time for self-examination. 🍎

Chinese Child Figures Weight of Elephant

The Chinese premier Tsao Tsao, in the late Han dynasty (early second century), one day received an elephant as a gift.

Out of curiosity, he wanted to know the weight of the huge animal, but not one of his subordinates could figure out how to weigh the elephant, as there was no scale big enough to do the job in those days in China.

"It might weigh five thousand pounds," one official said.

"It might be double that," the other one answered.

There were many guesses, yet none could be proved. When the premier was about to give up, his six-year-old son, Tsao Tsung, approached him.

"Dad," the young boy said to his premier father, "I have an idea how to find out the elephant's weight."

Suddenly, the noisy hall became silent. Everyone, including the premier, listened to the very young man speak of the solution to the problem.

"It is simple," the boy announced with confidence. "Take the elephant to a large empty boat and mark a sign on the gunwale to see how deep it goes into the water. Then, take the animal back ashore and keep putting rocks on the boat until it reaches the mark. Weigh the rocks one by one, and the total weight of the rocks should be pretty much the weight of that huge elephant."

Premier Tsao was very happy to take his son's advice and easily got the answer.

Another Chinese man, who lived at Chu, once traveled by boat. In order to reach the destination earlier, he asked the boat's operators not to stop, even in the night.

While the boat was advancing, the man sat by the boat's edge to watch the beautiful moonlight reflecting on the river. Accidentally, he dropped his beloved sword into the river. It was almost midnight. The man immediately made a mark on the upper edge of the boat where his sword slipped down into the water. Then, he went back to sleep.

The next morning, when the sun rose high in the sky, and the boat reached the port, the man jumped down into the water to find the mark he had made the night before. He began to search for his lost sword. He was laughed at by all the people who discovered what he was doing.

These two persons did one thing identically, marking a sign on the gunwale of the boat to remember something important. But one person was praised as a very smart boy, while the other one was laughed at as an extremely stupid guy.

There are many similar instances. Because of differences in time, place, purpose, and conditions, some win applause, and others are blamed. Therefore, we should not follow another person's steps without cautious thinking. He did it. She did it. But it does not mean that you can do the same. For example, having a martini before a meal is not a bad idea for some people, but I cannot enjoy it at all; it would ruin my appetite. A careful judgment is needed at all times. 🍎

Mencius and His Mother's Unfinished Cloth

Mencius is one of the greatest Chinese philosophers, next only to Confucius.

When Mencius was very young, his father died. His mother tried every way she could to educate Mencius properly and strictly. When she noticed that her son was strongly imitating the neighbor's behavior, she realized the importance of environment. They moved three times and finally settled in a very nice school neighborhood. As a result, when young Mencius watched the diligent students study hard every day, he begged his mother to let him join them in the school. Consequently, he gained much knowledge, and his actions and deportment also became more refined.

Later, when Mencius became a teenager, his mother sent him to a well-known school faraway from home. Mencius had to live in the school dormitory. As everything was unfamiliar and inconvenient, he became very homesick.

One day he sneaked out of the school and secretly went back home without the knowledge of school authorities.

His mother was surprised by his unexpected

return. After learning the cause of his leaving school, the wise mother did not scold her son directly, but picked up a pair of scissors and went to the loom where she was weaving every day. Without a word, the mother suddenly cut the unfinished cloth on the loom in half.

"Mom! Why did you destroy the unfinished cloth? It must have taken you a long time to weave it." The young Mencius was confused.

"Why? My dear child," the mother explained in tears, "it should take you a long time to study in the best school we can afford. Now you quit the school when you are only half done. What is the difference between my cutting the unfinished cloth and your quitting the unfinished schooling?"

The young Mencius was indeed a smart boy. He immediately understood his mother's action and analogy. He knelt down in front of his mother and swore he would go back to school soon. He promised he would never quit again until he had finished his education.

This kind of home education made Mencius one of the greatest Chinese in history. 🐦

Small Drops of Water Can Become an Ocean

Since China is the most populated nation in the world, the feeding of millions of people has always been the most urgent policy of the Chinese government, no matter who rules the country.

There are many more farmers in China than in any other nation. Since rice is the main food in the Chinese meal, millions of Chinese farmers grow rice.

Is it easy to plant a paddy of rice? My business partner, Peter Chen, as a young boy, helped his family grow rice years ago in Taiwan. According to Peter, there was just too much work to do before the raw, white grains of rice were put into the sack. There was no farm machinery in those days in Taiwan. Hard work and diligence were the only secrets to growing more rice. For thousands of years, nobody ever thought of a "shortcut" except one Chinese farmer.

In the Chinese classic, *Meng Tzu*, a farmer once went to the field to work early in the morning by himself. In the later afternoon, he returned home and happily told his wife that he had "helped" the rice sprouts grow. What he really did was pull each sprout a little bit higher to make his rice sprouts appear taller than those in his neighbor's field. He was proud of his smart way of planting. The next day, when he went back to his paddy field, he was surprised to find that all of his rice sprouts had totally decayed.

Meng Tzu is also known as Mencius, 372 B.C. to 289 B.C. He told his disciples the previous story to remind them that there was no "shortcut" in the growing of rice or in the studies of the classics.

I have never forgotten the meaningful remarks of my respectable adviser, Professor Wang Shu-min, when I was a freshman at National Taiwan University. He said that there was positively no "shortcut" in the field of Chinese literature studies. "Small tiny drops of water can gradually become an ocean. Tiny grains of sand can eventually turn into a vast land. All great, successful scholars had years of hard, continuous studies."

As my middle age is gradually leaving me, and the new life of "senior citizen" is slowly coming toward me, I now further believe that success in any profession is like the growing of rice and the study of classical literature. 🍒

Priceless Treasures

A pictorial had movie actress Elizabeth Taylor as its cover girl. She was wearing expensive earrings and necklace, a 33.19-carat diamond ring on her finger, and a $1.5 million bracelet on her wrist. The magazine article told the history of each piece of jewelry given to her by her former husbands. The article described in detail the jewelry and its present value, as if giving a display of a successful woman's treasures. The writer of the article failed to mention, however, that Liz's beauty was actually her most priceless treasure.

I also read a Chinese newspaper column about the lives of the four outstanding Chinese-American scientists who won Nobel Prizes in the fields of physics and chemistry in the past few decades. They all had their undergraduate studies in China and Taiwan and graduate studies in the United States. According to their families, they still spent most of their time in the lab and seldom sought pleasure for themselves. For them, the results of their research were their priceless treasure, which made them proud.

An old Chinese man once tried to bribe a judge with his heirloom, a piece of rare jade, as the old man's only son had broken the law and would be punished by going to jail.

"This is a very priceless treasure. I hope you like it," the old man said to the judge.

"This piece of rare jade is indeed a priceless treasure of yours," the judge told the old man very seriously. "But integrity is my priceless treasure. If I take your jade, you will lose your treasure, and I shall lose mine, too. Let us both keep our own treasures. Please take your jade back."

A scholarly Buddhist monk caught a thief who could not find any valuables in the temple.

"How could you not have any valuable things in your temple?" the thief asked. "Everyone says you have treasures."

"I do have a treasure." The monk smiled and said, "My sincere belief in Buddhism is my most priceless treasure."

Every person hopes to have a treasure. What do you hope to be your priceless treasure? 🍒

The Ghost of Suspicion

A wealthy Chinese man in Hong Kong married a pretty female salesclerk.

He had a few successful enterprises, which made him busy all the time, so he often returned home quite late. His wife quit her low-income job after marriage and stayed at home. Because they had no child, there was not much housework. She felt lonely most of the time, especially when he called her telling her he could not come home for supper. She was not happy, but she could do nothing about it.

Gradually, the unpleasantness mixed with loneliness turned into suspicion. She suspected her husband might have a secret sweetheart. Upon returning to her parents' home, she discussed the suspicion with her mother. The sophisticated mother warned her daughter not to fight with the husband, as fighting could only make things worse.

The mother advised that hiring a private detective might be worthwhile to try. Since there was no better solution, the young wife took the suggestion.

A couple of months later, the detective still could not supply her with evidence of her husband's disloyalty. She had to pay quite expensive detective fees.

Soon, the smart businessman-husband found out about the big mysterious payment. He traced his wife's footsteps and surprisingly found that she was secretly dating an unfamiliar handsome man at a high-class restaurant. He was a stubborn man who did not want to consult anybody else over his private matter. He went to a bar after office hours, trying to figure out the best resolution by himself, but he could not find one. The more he went to bars, the worse his life became.

The husband and wife started to argue and to fight. They were entering a "cold war." Finally, after a severe fight, they both decided to file for divorce. After they had signed the last legal document, they found they missed each other very much; but it was too late, since she had already moved out of his house.

One warm, sunny, late afternoon, the young lady drove to a lakeside and went for a quiet walk. It was the place where she and her former husband used to spend many lovely hours. The lake was still charming, and the wind was still soft, but she was extremely lonely. There was nobody else at the lake except a few birds flying around the aquatic plants. The whole world stood still. Suddenly, she discovered a person sitting against a large tree facing the calm water. Obviously, the person was in profound meditation and did not notice her approaching. Soon she found that it was her newly divorced husband.

You probably know what happened next. The

couple remarried. They swore they would never suspect each other again. She would not have to pay to "date" a handsome private detective in exchange for information about her husband's social activities, and he would do his best to return home for supper with his lonely wife.

Let me tell you another story, a sad one this time.

A Chinese coward once walked on a wild mountain road by himself at night. He could see nobody else. Under the cold moonlight, he noticed that a monster was closely following him step by step. So he started to run as fast as he could.

Unfortunately, he could not escape the untouchable ghost. Finally he died of exhaustion and fright, frightened to death by his own shadow.

A popular Chinese proverb says, "Suspicion raises dark ghost." Suspicion killed the man on the road and almost ruined the marriage of a Hong Kong couple.

Can we trust each other without unreasonable suspicion? ❦

The Bottle of Happiness

Many women envied her. She was young, pretty, and well educated. She was from a wealthy family and had married a handsome, successful business-man. But she was not happy. She even once thought of committing suicide.

After the wedding ceremony, she and her husband flew from Taiwan, where they were born and raised, to Paris, to spend their honeymoon. They happily visited almost every country in Europe, including Russia and some former communist nations. They had a wonderful time. She admitted she was one of the luckiest women in the world.

Soon after they returned to Taiwan, he went back to work. He worked for a prosperous trading company that his father founded years ago.

Since they were wealthy people, he agreed she could quit her teacher's job, which she never liked anyway. She stayed at home as a housewife.

Her husband was the eldest child of his parents. Following the traditional Chinese custom, the cou-ple lived with his parents. He had one younger brother and two younger sisters. They were still high-school students and lived at home, too.

From the beginning, it seemed that the young

newly wedded wife could not get along very well with her authoritative parents-in-law. Furthermore, she thought his brother and sisters disliked her. She hated to live with them. She wanted to move out with her husband and establish their own home. But the head of the family, her father-in-law, strongly objected.

The only person in the big family who would happily communicate with her was her husband. They deeply loved each other, and he tried every way he could to please her, except to move out of his parents' home. He was a traditionally filial Chinese son, reluctant to disobey his parents.

A few months later, the newly wedded couple started to argue. She complained that he was not as considerate as he used to be. He also thought she was not as reasonable as she had been before marriage.

She was depressed, yet she did not know how to improve the situation. One day, after a quarrel, she even thought of committing suicide. But the next day, when he showed her his sincere love, she had hope again.

It was Friday. The husband had earlier promised his wife he would take her out for dinner and dancing at a private club that weekend. In the late afternoon, he called from his office to tell her that he must fly to Los Angeles that night to negotiate important business on behalf of his sick father, the president of the company. He would stay in the United States probably for three or four days.

The sudden cancellation of their scheduled activities was a disappointment. She realized the importance of company business, but she still was very upset.

After seeing her husband off at the airport, she drove her imported Mercedes along the streets with no particular destination but to pass the time. Suddenly, she was attracted by a small sign on a Buddhist temple. She remembered a long time ago that her aged grandmother liked to visit the temple. Out of curiosity, she stopped in front of the temple and walked inside.

It was indeed an old Buddhist temple. The main hall needed repairs. The walls needed repainting. A few doors had been partially damaged. There were only two nuns there. Both of them looked very peaceful and pleasant. They welcomed her sincerely and warmly. She had an unexpected joyful time with them. From that time on, she became a frequent visitor at the temple.

Unexpectedly, the frequent meetings with the two nuns caused her to change the rest of her life.

According to the nuns, she had a bottle of happiness. Her biggest enemy was actually "herself." She had used the ideology of "me" to choke the bottle, so her happiness could not come out. Once she married her husband, she thought his parents should like her, his younger brother and sisters should respect her, and, of course, her husband should love her and be at her side all the time. She never thought of others or cared about them. She only blamed other people for not treating her well. She would not blame herself for not treating others well. It was so simple. Her happiness was right there in the bottle, but she never opened it and choked it with "me."

Having this interpretation, she returned home and started to care for her husband's parents and brother and sisters. She quit blaming others and often examined whether she had cared for other people enough. The sudden change finally brought back the happiness that she used to have.

Everyone has happiness; happiness is always there, but only if you know how to use it. 🍃

The Bell on the Tiger's Neck

The tiger is supposedly a dangerous, wild animal. No person dares approach a tiger except a wild animal trainer. But even though he is an experienced animal trainer, he would not pat a tiger's shoulder if he happened to meet the animal in the woods.

That is the reason the Chinese people often describe a dangerous job by saying, "It is like striking a fly on a tiger's head."

Since nobody can strike a fly on a tiger's head, how do we untie the bell that is hanging on a tiger's neck? One day, a group of Chinese Buddhist monks discussed this question.

"I would untie the bell while the tiger is in deep sleep," one monk said.

"If I were given such a job," another monk announced, "I would feed the tiger first. If a tiger is full, he might not hurt people as much as he would when hungry. Then, I would try to approach him and untie the bell from his neck."

"None of your methods are absolutely safe," an old monk insisted. "The best way is to bind the tiger tightly with a very strong rope. We have to make sure the tiger can't hurt people. Then, I would go ahead and untie the bell."

"Who would bind the tiger?" asked a young monk. No one answered.

Finally, they went to their chief monk, Tai Chin, who was well known for solving hard questions. After hearing the question and all the answers, monk Tai Chin laughed and declared, "The person who put the bell on the tiger's neck is the right person to take down the bell from the tiger's neck. He is the only one who knows how to do it well without risk."

The message of this story is still practical in China. When we face a very complicated problem, and no one knows how to solve it, it is often suggested that the person who started the problem should know how to solve it.

Can we use this same Oriental philosophy to help us find solutions to perplexities in the world today? 🐿

Acorns for the Monkeys

Chuang-tzu, a great Chinese philosopher who lived more than 2,400 years ago, told a story about a man who was very fond of monkeys.

At this man's home, he fed and took good care of many monkeys every day, treating the animals almost like his own children. It was said that he might even be able to communicate with his monkeys.

One day, when he found that he could not afford to buy enough food for the monkeys, he told them he was having a hard time making money. He decided to reduce the food portion for each monkey to three acorns in the morning and four in the evening.

The monkeys were not happy. They lay on the ground in protest. The man then asked his animals, "If you don't like it this way, shall we change it to four acorns in the morning and three in the evening?"

As the number of nuts in the beginning of the day increased from three to four, the monkeys accepted the deal and jumped up and down in agreement.

Since the total number of nuts was the same, and there was actually no essential difference between the "three in the morning, four in the evening" and the "four in the morning, three in the evening," the monkeys were fooled by the so-called outward form. What the Chinese philosopher tried to advise us is that when the politicians promise changes, we should not be tricked by visual changes, but should examine the change in essence. 🐌

A Chinese Man
Who Had Two Wives

About 2,400 years ago, in a kingdom called Chu in east-central China, there was a businessman who had two wives. Both were pretty women. (In old China, a man could marry as many women as he wanted and could afford.)

The man had to make out-of-town business trips quite often. Sometimes, he could not return home for more than a week. Therefore, the two young wives felt lonely while their husband was gone.

Their next-door neighbor was a handsome bachelor who tried to take advantage of the husband's absences. He invited the two beautiful women out for dinner. The older woman knew the neighbor's wicked intention and coolly turned down the invitation immediately, but the naive younger woman accepted it with pleasure.

As time went on, their secret dates continued, and finally, the neighbor and the younger woman had an affair. Gradually, almost all of the neighbors became aware of it except the poor man with two wives.

A year later, the husband died in an accident.

The two wives suddenly became helpless. It gave the neighbor a good opportunity.

Everyone thought the bachelor neighbor would marry the younger widow, his secret sweetheart. Surprisingly, the neighbor married the older widow and absolutely rejected the younger one's begging.

The neighbor was cruelly blamed by all the people who knew about their relationship. "Why?" he logically explained. "Every man hopes his wife will be loyal to him under any condition. I just don't want my wife to be easily seduced by a handsome man while I am away from home."

Today, polygamy is prohibited in America, China, and most other nations. But "the neighbor," "the older wife," and "the younger wife" can still be found almost in every place, in any time, and often without awareness. ❧

A Story of Chiang Ching-kuo in Taiwan

Chiang Ching-kuo was the former president of the Republic of China in Taiwan. Before becoming the president, he was the prime minister.

One day, when Chiang and some of his followers were making an inspection trip through a small town, they stopped at a tiny café for supper. Chiang found that the only two workers in the shop were arguing. They were brothers and partners in the café. Their last name was Fong. The elder brother was a very good manager and bookkeeper, as well as waiter, and the younger one was an excellent cook. They were making a good living. But they could not get along very well, and they planned to dissolve the partnership and close the business.

After learning the whole story, Chiang ordered a bowl of beef noodles. When the bowl was set on the table, Chiang used one chopstick to try to pick up the long Chinese noodles from his bowl to eat, but he could not pick up anything. The Fong brothers soon came over and said to Chiang, "Mr. Prime Minister, you should use two chopsticks to pick up the noodles."

Chiang Ching-kuo took the advice and quickly

ate his noodles with two chopsticks. Then he asked the two brothers to sit down next to him. He spoke to them, "Of course, I know how to use chopsticks to eat. When two chopsticks cooperate with each other, a person can get food to eat. The two chopsticks hit each other sometimes, but they never dissolve their partnership, because they know the importance of cooperation."

After the meal, Chiang and his group paid the bill and left the café without saying any more.

The two brothers finally changed their minds. They would not dissolve their partnership, and they cooperated with each other more closely. The Fong brothers are now successful businessmen. They bought a big building and turned it into a bigger restaurant with many employees.

I never had a chance to meet Chiang. When he took power in Taiwan, I had already immigrated to this country.

Taiwan is a small island of only 13,836 square miles, but less than one-seventh the area of state of Wyoming. But Chiang Ching-kuo made Taiwan one of the richest nations in the world. He died in 1988, but his wisdom will always be a worthy memorial to the Chinese people, including the Fong brothers, in Taiwan. 🍎

A Clever Plan

One of the Aesop's fables tells about a thirsty crow who found a pitcher with some water in it. But so little water was there that, try as she might, she could not reach it with her beak. It seemed as though she would die of thirst within sight of the remedy.

At last, she hit upon a clever plan. She began dropping pebbles into the pitcher, and with each pebble dropped, the water rose a little higher. Finally, it reached the brim, and the smart bird was able to quench her thirst.

In the Chinese Sung dynasty of the tenth century, a young boy by the name of Wen Yuan-po was playing with his companions, chasing a ball under a tall tree. Suddenly, the ball dropped into a hole by the roots of the tree. It was not a big hole, but big enough to hold the ball. It was not too deep, as the kids could still see the ball, but none of the boys' hands were long enough to touch the ball.

They tried every way to pick up the ball, but in vain. That was the only ball they had, so the boys would not give up. One boy used a broken branch, and it touched the ball, but the ball was still left at the bottom of the hole.

Finally, Wen "hit upon a clever plan" and carried over a bucket of water. He poured the water right into the hole. Before half of the bucket of water had been used, the ball floated on the water, and Wen easily picked it up. The smart boy later became a successful Chinese prime minister who ruled China for almost four decades.

These two stories are quite different from each other, but they have one key point in common. Both the crow and the boy know how to use something else besides their own energies to achieve their purposes.

Have you ever noticed that many successful people make their way to success by the same means that the bird and the boy used? 🐦

The Finest Steed

Many years ago, a Chinese king was fond of horses. His dream was to have the finest steed in the world. Although he had many gentle horses in his palace, none of them met his qualifications as the world's best horse. So the king kept looking for horses. He told his officials that he would do whatever he could to obtain such a steed.

A king in those days of ancient China had absolute power to do whatever he wished. Many merciless kings did cruel things to get what they wanted. Therefore, the people who owned fine horses would not let their king or even the king's officials know their secret. They were not sure how high a price the king would pay for a fine steed. If the king liked the horse, but would not pay the price the horse owner wanted, the owner could do nothing about it, and the fine horse might be taken by the king anyway.

Three years passed. The king was still looking for the finest steed in the world.

One day, a lower official came to see the king. He said if he could have 500 gold coins, he was sure he could help the king obtain a fine steed. The king gave the man the money.

A couple of months later, the young official returned to the king's palace with a heavy package. He reported to the king that he had finally found a very fine steed, but the horse was dead already. So, he paid the horse's master 500 gold coins to cut off the horse's head. He brought it back in a wooden case.

The king was very angry. He said that he wanted a live steed, not a dead one. A dead horse's head was worth nothing, no matter how fine the horse used to be. The king ordered severe punishment. Then the lower official hastily reported to the king again, "When I paid the owner of the dead horse 500 gold coins, I told him that our king would pay many times that amount if he could buy a live one. Therefore, I am sure we shall have many people coming to the palace, bringing their fine steeds to sell."

The official was right. Within three months, many people in the kingdom and some even from other nations came to the king's palace with their fine horses.

The king finally bought the finest steed of his dreams. The lower official gained both a big promotion and the king's confidence. 🦋

Confidence Is Something Bewitching

┌═╗┌═╗ ┌═╗┌═╗ ┌═╗┌═╗ ┌═╗┌═╗ ┌═╗┌═╗ ┌═╗┌═╗ ┌═╗┌═╗

Bewitched was one of my favorite television shows. In one episode, when the hero Darrin's project was not accepted by his client, he went home in very low spirits. He suspected that his witch mother-in-law must have cast a bad spell on him again, as she often did.

The heroine, his pretty witch/wife, Samantha, quickly made a thorough investigation and found that none of her witch family had caused anything to happen to her mortal husband this time. Instead, she told her discouraged husband that she had just put a good spell on him to make sure he would get along smoothly with his client and his boss when he returned to the office.

Darrin, believing he was working with a good spell on him, forced his client and his boss to listen again to his full explanation of the project. Suddenly, the stubborn client changed his mind and happily accepted Darrin's work, as Darrin thought he would.

When Darrin returned home, his spirits lowered again. He told his wife that her witchcraft did work, but he was afraid that in the future he might have to rely on witchcraft, which he really hated.

Then Samantha told her husband the true story, that she had not put any spell on him. She deceived him to stimulate him to face the problem, and he solved it with his own ability. His confidence, not the witchcraft, made Darrin succeed. Without confidence, he would not have dared to force his client and his boss to listen to him again.

According to a noted Chinese educator, confidence produces courage, and courage is a necessity to make things work out. It works well in business, as Darrin proved. It applies to military affairs, too.

In the middle of the eleventh century, a Chinese general named Ti Ching once led his troops to battle. Midway, the soldiers heard that the number of enemy soldiers was several times bigger than theirs, so the boys were frightened and nervous. Suddenly, the military morale was terribly low.

Soon, the army passed by a Buddhist temple. Ti Ching told his men that he would pray to Buddha for help, so he went into the temple by himself. When he came out, he announced that Buddha indicated they must make their own decisions by throwing coins.

Ti Ching pulled ten coins out of his pocket and tossed them up into the air. According to Buddha's indication, if the ten coins fell on the ground with the same pattern up, it meant that they would definitely win the battle no matter how big the enemy was. If the ten coins had different patterns, they had better retreat and wait for another chance.

To the great surprise and cheers of the soldiers, the patterns of all ten coins were exactly the same. General Ti Ching picked up his coins and led his army to the battlefield in high spirits. They won the war.

Actually, only General Ti Ching knew that his coins were fake, with the same patterns on both sides. Confidence made them win the battle. The smart Chinese general used a trick to fortify his army's confidence.

What is confidence? It cannot be seen, touched, or smelled. It is the kind of self-assurance that we must all have in order to get what we want. 🍎

How to Keep Your Appetite for Fish

Kung-sun I was a senior official of Lu, a kingdom in north-central China, about 2,600 years ago.

Because of his job responsibilities, Kung-sun saw the king almost every day, and he won the king's high trust. Therefore, many officials who wanted to approach the king, but hardly had a chance, came to Kung-sun begging for help.

Those people also learned that Kung-sun was very fond of eating fish, which was scarce in the capital, a mainland city. The price of fish was high, and there was often a shortage.

In order to please Kung-sun, many officials tried hard to get fish for him. They presented the fish to Kung-sun, asking him to make arrangements for them to see the king or asking him to say some favorable words for them. When this happened, Kung-sun always turned down the gift courteously, but emphatically.

He never accepted one fish from one person. But he went to the market and paid high prices for fish every day.

Kung-sun's son was confused. The boy had

noticed that each person left with disappointment when his father had refused to accept the fish.

"Dad," the boy asked, "since you love fish so much, and it is not easy to buy it at such high prices, why don't you accept the gifts and make both yourself and your friends happy?"

"My dear son," Kung-sun answered, "because I like to eat fish very much, I don't want to lose the delicious taste."

The answer perplexed the young man even more, so Kung-sun continued his explanation. "If I accepted the fish gift from a certain official, I would have to do something in return for him. If I could not arrange for him to see the king, I would have to say some favorable words on his behalf. Pretty soon, more and more people would bring me fish, and I would have to do favors for each of them, one by one. Eventually, our smart king would catch on to the trick. Then, I would be severely punished. Even if I were not executed, I would be put in jail. In that case, how would I keep my appetite for fish in prison? Since I have not accepted any gifts, I am not obligated to do anything for them. As long as I keep the job, I can buy fish with the good salary I make. I can enjoy my appetite all the time."

Kung-sun I's philosophy was, indeed, very simple, but many people just cannot follow it in every country and all the time. 🐦

How to Prepare
for the Role

Hollywood actress Victoria Principal prepared for her role as a blind woman in a movie by wearing a blindfold day and night for two weeks.

"I cooked and ate dinner blindfolded. I even tended to business at my office with my eyes covered," said the former star of the CBS show Dallas. "The most frightening part is in the mornings, because there is no way to prepare for waking up blind."

During filming in Utah, she wore special contact lenses that distorted her vision and made her legally blind, according to the news report.

Although I have not seen the movie, I would expect an excellent performance, as Victoria experienced what a blind woman would feel and how she would act during those two weeks.

Every kind of business and politics involves the same principle. If a politician does not understand the likes and dislikes of the majority, he will not have continual support of the people. The best ruler of a nation must come from the common people. The ruler must know what the people need and what they care about. Otherwise, the ruler will be cast out, sooner or later, as was the Chinese emperor Chin Hui-ti of the late third century.

Hui-ti was born in his emperor father's palace. When his father died, Hui-ti took over the position as the new emperor in China. But he knew nothing about his people. The worst thing was that he had no intention of knowing anything about them. When he received reports about drought and famine, with thousands of people starving to death, he was puzzled. One of his close officials told him that there were more and more people having no rice to eat. The careless ruler responded, "Since they don't have rice to eat, why don't they eat meatballs instead?"

The naive Chinese emperor liked to eat meatballs himself, but he never realized the price of meat and how hard it was to get any kind of food. He was later overthrown by his officials.

Chiang Kai-shek, the former president of the Chinese Nationalist government, with his large, well-equipped, modern army, lost all of mainland China to only a handful of poorly equipped Chinese Communists in 1949. One of the reasons for Chiang's failure was that he had not had direct contact with the common people for a long time. For example, when China experienced dramatic inflation because of many years of war, most Chinese officials could not support their families with the income they received from Chiang's government. But Chiang still thought he was paying the officials enough to make a good living. He lost his people's support first; then he was driven out of the China mainland.

An outstanding actor or actress, such as Victoria Principal, must completely understand the way of life for the role he or she is going to portray. Then a convincing picture can be presented to the audience.

A respectable politician, especially a president, also has to understand his role. Without knowing how much a common citizen makes, how much rice costs, or which is less expensive, rice or meatballs, the ruler will have to be overthrown. 🍎

Surprising Growth of
Some Seeds

In the northern part of the province of Kiang-su, China, there was a Buddhist temple on a deserted road of a city. Two monks lived there. The older monk named Huan-hsu was the younger monk's teacher.

On Sunday or certain Buddhist occasions, the temple was always crowded with many adherents. But on the ordinary weekdays, it was quiet. Because of no plants growing around the temple, it made the lone building look more monotonous.

In a Sunday meeting, an adherent suggested growing some plants in front of the temple. The suggestion met unanimous agreement. In a few days, the monks received donations of many sacks of plant seeds.

The two monks took the seeds outside. They planted the seeds in front of their temple as carefully as they could.

A couple of days later, an unexpected strong wind came. It blew out almost everything outside of the buildings. After the wind, the monks went out to check what they had planted. They found that most of the seeds had been blown away. The young monk was very sad. But the old monk comforted him saying that since they had done their part, there should be no regret.

A few days later, a storm suddenly came. After the storm, the flood was as high as two feet. When the flood finally retreated, the monks rechecked their gardening and could find no seeds left at the place they planted. The young monk was so upset that he wanted to cry. But the old monk said that as both the strong wind and the storm were beyond their control, they should not feel regretful.

A month later, the young monk was overjoyed to find that thousands of saplings were coming out of the ground all around the building. A year later, the temple stood like in a beautiful garden.

Monk Huan-hsu told his student monk, "Like growing the plants, since we have done our best, we should not feel too sad if we do not see the immediate results. When the results come to us unexpectedly, we should not feel too excitedly, either." 🐾

Opportunity May Not Come Again

As everybody knows, monkeys like to eat fruit. An old female monkey took her three sons to travel. They traveled from one mountain to the other with high interest. Finally, they got lost. And the worst thing was that they could not find any kind of fruit or nuts or anything to eat. It was a bald mountain. And it was in a winter.

Being awfully hungry, the mother monkey led her children to kneel down to pray. They begged the Mighty Lord to give them a chance to survive.

Soon after they stood up, a miracle appeared. A peach orchard suddenly showed up right in front of them. A gardener walked out of the orchard, inviting the monkeys to go inside. The gardener told them that each of them could pick a peach to eat. They could choose the peaches as big as they wanted, but each monkey could pick one peach only.

Another rule was that the monkeys could only go ahead and could not retreat or turn back their heads. When they reached the exit in the back of the orchard, they must get out without hesitation.

The four hungry monkeys were very happy to

enter into the orchard, and they surely found many peaches hanging on each tree. As each of them was permitted to pick one peach only, they tried their best to choose a bigger one without flaws. Soon the mother monkey and her two older sons had found their favorite peaches and finished eating and happily left the orchard from its back door. But the youngest monkey followed his mother and brothers to go out of the orchard unhappily.

He told his mother and brothers that in the beginning, he did find many big peaches. But, as he could only be allowed to pick one peach, he examined each big peach as carefully as he could and found that every one had some kind of flaw. So he kept going with a hope that maybe he would see a perfect big one further ahead. Unfortunately, he did not find any better one until he saw the sign of exit. He could not retreat, but followed his mother and brothers to get out.

After the monkeys told each other their stories, they were surprised to find that the peach orchard had disappeared completely.

Opportunities come and go. When an opportunity comes to a person, if the person thinks that it is not the perfect one he wants and hopes a better one will come in the future and lets the opportunities pass away one after the other, one of these days, the person will be mostly like the above young monkey getting out of the orchard with an empty stomach. 🍑

We Sometimes Cross Solid Lines

Somewhere in China, there was a Buddhist temple built on a high mountain. The Buddhist monks planted their own vegetables and some corn, so they did not have any problem getting food, as a Buddhist monk is supposed to be a strict vegetarian.

They went to a nearby town by the foot of the mountain to buy some necessities every few months. Because the older monks always did the shopping, the younger monks never had a chance to see the other kind of world. Consequently, the youngsters did not meet people, other than the monks in the temple.

One day, it was the turn of an old monk to do the regular shopping. He was not feeling very well, and he took his teenage student monk with him as the student could help the teacher carry the stuff. In the town, the young monk was very excited to see so many interesting things and people, especially the colorfully dressed women. (The Buddhist monks have to wear the grey and brown monk uniforms year-round.)

"What kind of people are they?" The student pointed to a few carefree young girls.

Because a Buddhist monk, like a Catholic priest, is not allowed to marry and he has to live an ascetic life, strictly repressive of any lustful desire, the old monk was afraid that his young student might be enticed to break the Buddhist rules and simply answered his student, "They are all dangerous vampires. Don't approach them."

The next day, when the two monks returned to their temple in the high mountains, all the other young monks secretly asked the young monk, who had just traveled the other kind of world, what was the most beautiful and interesting stuff he had seen in town. Without any hesitation, the young monk answered, "the vampires."

Here is another story about Buddhist monks and women. Once an old Buddhist monk, accompanied by his young student monk, was trying to cross a river, but they could not find any ferry and ferryman.

At the same time, there came a pretty young woman who was very eager to cross the river, too. The girl cried that she had to return to her home on the other side of the river before the sun set. The old monk offered the very delicate lady his help. He carried the pretty girl on his back and crossed the shallow river on foot.

A couple of months later, the student monk could not repress his emotion anymore. He mentioned this happening to his teacher and asked confusedly, "As Buddhist monks, you always teach us not to touch any woman in order to stick to our Buddhist rules. How could you carry a young pretty girl on your back two months ago?"

The old monk smiled and replied to his student very wisely, "I did carry a woman on the back to cross a shallow river as she had to return home that afternoon and there was no ferryman around. Soon after I put her down on the ground on the other side of river, my 'load' was released completely. My poor student, how could you still carry the heavy 'load' in your mind for more than two months?"

Personally, I prefer the old monk in the second story. A great statesman said, "You can deceive a person for a while, but you cannot do it to all of the persons forever." All kinds of rules are still but rules. Normally nobody can break the rules. But occasionally, we have to drive on a double solid line in order to avoid a more dangerous accident. More importantly, we must face the reality and tell the truth, especially when we are educating the youngsters. Therefore, I don't like the way the old monk did it in the first story.

We Can Be Happy About Who We Are

Nobody knows when and how it started, but a cat always likes to chase a mouse, no matter when and where. Therefore, mice all hate cats very much, and they try hard to look for powerful helps to fight against their enemies.

Once upon a time somewhere in China, a pair of mice decided to find a good match for their only child, a young, pretty female mouse, as the Chinese parents of human beings always did for the children. Because of hatred of cats, the mice tried to find a very powerful creature other than a young male mouse as their son-in-law to get revenge on the cats.

When the mouse father was walking outside in search of a powerful creature to match with his daughter, the sun hung on the sky, with his heat making everyone feel he was the most powerful creature in the universe. So the mouse father proposed marriage to the sun with his daughter.

The sun honestly told the old male mouse that he was not actually the most powerful creature. The cloud often came to block his heat. So he suggested the mouse ask the cloud.

Soon, the cloud admitted that when he was blocking the heat of sun, the wind often came to blow him away. So he advised the mouse to see the wind.

But the wind sighed first, then replied that it was true he was not weak, but whenever he met the wall, he just could not go through.

So the mouse visited the wall, telling him the reason why he had come. After hearing all the stories of visits, the wall told the old mouse that in his opinion, the mice themselves should be the most powerful creatures, because the mice often made holes at the bottom of walls as the places to live while the walls just could not resist. In early China, most walls were made of mud.

After all the visits, the old male mouse had to tell his wife that they had really no choice but to marry their daughter to a young male mouse, although they would still be afraid of cats.

The above Chinese tale tells us that nobody is absolutely the most powerful person, and nothing is actually perfect. We all admire the persons who hold big power in their hands and the persons who have lots of money. But as powerful as is the president of a nation, he is always afraid of being assassinated; and a billionaire is afraid of being kidnapped, too. As long as we are careful enough not to be attacked by "cats," we can all be happy of who we are. 🐾

How Awful When Rumors Fly

▨▨▨▨▨▨▨▨▨▨▨▨▨▨

Tseng Shen also known as Tseng-tzu (505 B.C.— 437 B.C.) was the greatest Chinese sage, one of Confucius's most outstanding students. He was also his mother's most filial son. When Tseng Shen was a boy, he was already very prudent in the way of doing things, and he won his mother's high confidence.

One day, when his mother was weaving cloth at home like most other Chinese housewives did in those years, a neighbor suddenly walked in saying, "A very bad news to you, Mrs. Tseng. I have just heard that your son killed a person."

"Thank you very much for your information," Tseng Shen's mother answered calmly without even stopping her weaving. "I know my son. He would not do such a terrible thing. It must be a groundless rumor."

Soon after the neighbor left, a close relative of Tseng's family ran in and shouted, "It is horrible news. Tseng Shen had just killed a person. The government army is searching for him. Where is your son, Mrs. Tseng?"

"My son is studying at school. He should be home pretty soon." Mrs. Tseng stopped her job and answered the relative politely. "I have complete confidence in my son. He would not kill any person no matter what. It should be a great mistake."

Not too long after the second messenger had left, a government official, also a family friend of Tseng's family, came in a great hurry. He confirmed the news. It was not a rumor. Tseng Shen did kill a person. According to the law, the murderer's family would be involved and severely punished, too. The friend suggested Mrs. Tseng find a place to hide at the moment.

Tseng Shen's mother was shocked this time. Three persons had said the same thing. She stood up and tried to discuss with the friend what she was supposed to do. Just at this moment, Tseng Shen returned home. He told his worrying mother that a person with the same name as his, also called Tseng Shen, killed a person by accident. The killer had been arrested.

A Chinese proverb says, "A rumor will quit in front of a wise person." Tseng Shen's mother was said in the records to be a wise lady. Yet, she was still suspicious of what she had been told by a series of three persons on a groundless rumor. What an awful impact a rumor can bring forth! 🐛

Writer Has to Study Hard

In the tenth century in northern China, there was a boy, Fang Chung-yung, who could write poems when he was five years old. Everybody in the family and neighborhood said that the boy was a genius. His parents were proud of him. The family was a wealthy one, but the boy's parents did not receive much education and thus were often looked down upon by the educated people in the area. Now their five year old was a genius! The father took his son to see the local most knowledgeable man and showed him the boy's works. The man agreed, too, that Fang was a genius.

With such praise in mind, Fang's father took Fang to the capital of the nation and many other big cities. The father tried to show his son's poems to as many intellects of the age as he could find. Naturally, they won many more praises. Because of traveling on the road, also mainly because of having received so many praises, Fang's father did not send his son back to school. "My boy is a genius already. Why should he go back to school?" the father said to his family. They were all intoxicated with Fang's being a genius.

Finally, they met Wang An-shek in the capital. Wang was supposed to be the most well-known scholar and poet in the nation. After reading Fang's poems, Wang told Fang's father that according to the age, he had to agree that the poems were good enough. But he advised the boy be sent to school to study hard. Unfortunately, Fang's father did not take the advice. He said to himself that since his son was a genius now, he should be a genius always.

Ten years later, Wang had a chance to read Fang's latest poems. He found that the boy's talent had not improved.

Another ten years later, when Wang read Fang's poems, he was sorry to tell his friends that he could not find any talent in the boy's works at all.

One of the few most outstanding Chinese-American writers, C.Y. Lee, the author of many best-selling English novels including *Flower Drum Song*, said on many occasions that a writer's talent might contribute to his writing one-tenth or two-tenths at the most, while hard work accounts for the rest of success. Without years and years of continuous writing, a person could never become a successful writer.

I agree heartily and completely. 🦋

Causes of Longevity

Since the newspapers published the story of a French woman, Jeanne Calment, whose greatest proven age of 120 gave her the title "the oldest person ever to live on the planet," many other very old persons have been found and reported from all around the world, according to a special report in a Chinese newspaper.

A Chinese woman named Rung Ying in Canton passed away last July at the age of 123, and a Chinese man in Hu-pei Province is still alive at 132.

In Syria, a man died a year ago at 133, and in the United Arab Emirates, a man was seen three years ago claiming he was 152 years old. Except Jeanne Calment, it seems that all of the other long-lived persons' ages can hardly be proven.

Among the nations, Japan is the one with much more long-lived persons than any other country. Presently, there are more than 4,800 Japanese people whose ages all pass 100.

A Chinese longevity expert studied the cause of longevity for years and gave his findings to the public. Although there are practically no real secrets for a person to live longer than 100 years, there are still some "ways" collected from the interviews of these long-lived people.

The most common "way" is that the person of longevity, no matter rich or poor, success or failure, man or woman, is easy to be satisfied with the present, optimistic for the future, and consequently often smiles when dealing with others. These long-lived people never deliberately demand to live to 100 years old or longer, but longevity comes to them unexpectedly.

The studies further warn us that it is true that easy to be satisfied, optimistic for the future, and smiling are the causes and the longevity is the result, but the three causes must come up naturally and sincerely. If you just want to live longer and you pretend you are satisfied, optimistic, and make smiles as an actor does, it will not work.

As a matter of fact, if everybody can practice the above three "ways," even just pretending, all of the crimes, the violence, and the cruel evilness will definitely be decreasing year after year. In that case, longevity is not very important, but a happy by-product. ❦

A Dog Named Time

An old Chinese man's wife got sick and died. He and his wife had been married for more than half a century. They never had children.

After the old companion was gone, the man felt very lonely. He took a friend's advice and bought a baby dog from a pet store. It was a miniature size of poodle which had long, thick, and frizzy hair. Everybody said it was a cute puppy. The old man treasured it very much and named his dog "Time."

When he sat, he often put the puppy on his knees. When he took a walk outside his house, he would put the dog down and ask it to follow him. Because the dog was only a few weeks old, it could not walk as fast as its master. So the man often called, "Go faster, Time." The little puppy had done its best. No matter how he called, it was still doing the same.

As time went by, the puppy became stronger. Like a little boy, it seldom stayed in one place too long. It ran around the house almost all the time. And it would not listen to its master as closely as it used to. Especially when the man took his dog outside to take a walk, the dog started to run faster than its master. So the man had to call, "Go slower,

Time." But no matter how the man called, it just would not slow down.

As time kept going on and on, finally the man became older and weaker, and the dog grew bigger and stronger. One day, when the man took his dog for a walk, he lost control of his dog, which ran far-away. The man kept calling, "Wait for me, Time." But Time just ran and would not listen to him.

Finally, the man realized that he really could not control the time. ❦

About the Author

Tom Ma was born on a large traditional Chinese farm in the northern province of Kiang-su, almost the center of China's east coast. He was the fifteenth generation of the Ma family to live in that particular area for nearly 300 years. With the takeover of the mainland by the Chinese Communists, Mr. Ma and his family were forced off their land. Mr. Ma graduated from National Taiwan University and then moved on to Western Michigan University. He currently lives with his family in Riverton, Wyoming, and is a frequent contributor to the *Riverton Ranger* newspaper.